2-06

D0794578

THE SKIN

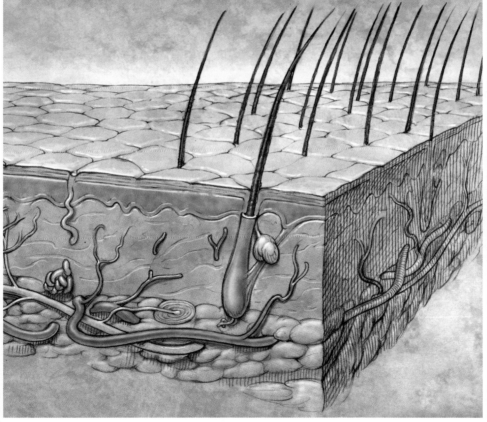

By Susan H. Gray

THE CHILD'S WORLD®
CHANHASSEN, MINNESOTA

The Child's World

Published in the United States of America by The Child's World
PO Box 326, Chanhassen, MN 55317-0326
800-599-READ
www.childsworld.com

Content Adviser:
R. John Solaro,
PhD, Distinguished
University Professor
Head, Department
of Physiology and
Biophysics, University
of Illinois at Chicago

Photo Credits: Cover/frontispiece: Photodisc. Interior: Custom Medical Stock Photo: 9 (B. Wainwright), 10 (K. Wood); Frank Lane Picture Agency/Corbis: 21; Getty Images: 6 (Photographer's Choice/Jack Ambrose), 14 (The Image Bank/Ryan McVay), 18 (Hulton|Archive); Getty Images/Photodisc: 16 (Todd Pearson), 25 (Russell Illig); Getty Images/Taxi: 7 (Michael Denora), 12 (Allan H. Shoemake), 13 (Stephen Simpson), 27 (Tony Anderson); Michael Newman/PhotoEdit: 19, 26; PhotoEdit: 5 (Tony Freeman), 15 (Frank Siteman), 22 (Myrleen Ferguson Cate).

The Child's World: Mary Berendes, Publishing Director

Editorial Directions, Inc.: E. Russell Primm, Editorial Director; Pam Rosenberg, Editor; Katie Marsico, Associate Editor; Judith Shiffer, Assistant Editor; Matt Messbarger, Editorial Assistant; Susan Hindman, Copy Editor; Sarah E. De Capua, Proofreader; Judith Frisbie, Peter Garnham, Olivia Nellums, Chris Simms, Fact Checkers; Tim Griffin/IndexServ, Indexer; Cian Loughlin O'Day, Photo Researcher; Linda S. Koutris, Photo Editor

The Design Lab: Kathleen Petelinsek, Design; Kari Thornborough, Production Design

Library of Congress Cataloging-in-Publication Data
Gray, Susan Heinrichs.
 The skin / by Susan H. Gray.
    p. cm. — (The human body)
 Includes index.
 ISBN 1-59296-429-X (lib. bound : alk. paper) 1. Skin—Juvenile literature. I. Title.
 QP88.5.G73 2005
 612.7'9—dc22   2005000525

Table of Contents

CHAPTER ONE

4 Wrinkles Come and Go

CHAPTER TWO

7 What Is Skin?

CHAPTER THREE

10 The Epidermis

CHAPTER FOUR

14 The Dermis and Hypodermis

CHAPTER FIVE

19 Nails, Hair, and Glands

CHAPTER SIX

24 What Does the Skin Do?

28 Glossary

29 Questions and Answers about the Skin

29 Did You Know?

30 How to Learn More about the Skin

31 Common Skin Disorders

32 Index

WRINKLES COME AND GO

Maria held her breath and jumped into the pool. It was a sunny, hot day in August, and she wanted to go swimming as much as possible before school started.

Maria climbed out of the pool and dried off. She sat down and poured some sunblock into her hand. That's when she noticed the wrinkles. The skin on each fingertip was all crinkled up—even on her thumbs! She wondered why this always happened when she went swimming.

Maria didn't know that there are many dead cells in the top layer of her skin. Those cells act just like little sponges. They soak up water and increase in size. Living cells that are deeper in her skin do not soak up the water. They stay their normal size. The top, water-soaked layer is tightly attached to the layer underneath. As the top layer swells up, it cannot spread out, so it stays in place and becomes wrinkled.

Maria finished putting on the sunblock and then stayed out of the pool for awhile. Out in the air, the skin cells on her

Putting sunblock on your skin before you go swimming is a good idea. It helps protect your skin from the harmful rays of the sun. It will also help prevent you from getting a painful sunburn.

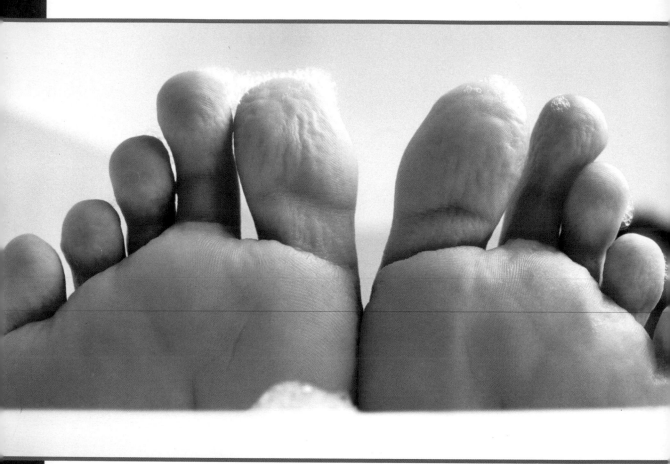

Your toes might look like this if you take a nice, long bath. But don't worry—as soon as they dry out, they'll be back to normal!

fingertips began to dry. They shrank down, and the wrinkles

disappeared. Maria looked at her fingertips again, and they

seemed normal. She wondered what on Earth was going on

with her skin!

CHAPTER TWO

WHAT IS SKIN?

Skin is the largest **organ** of the body. It separates the

organs and tissues on the inside of the body from the

environment that is outside the body. In other words, it holds all

the body tissues in, and it

keeps everything else out.

Skin has other jobs,

as well. It keeps our

bodies from drying out,

and it protects us against

infection. It allows us

to feel heat, cold, touch,

and pain. Skin helps

Skin is the largest organ of the human body. It keeps our insides in and helps keep germs out.

us get rid of waste materials. It also helps our bodies stay at the right temperature.

Skin has two main layers—the epidermis (EP-ih-DUR-miss) and the dermis (DUR-miss). The epidermis is a thin, outside layer. Just beneath it is the dermis, which is a thicker layer. Beneath the dermis is a fatty layer called the hypodermis (HI-poe-DUR-miss). Skin has different levels of thickness on different parts of the body. Eyelid skin is only about 0.02 inches (0.5 millimeters) thick, while skin on the back is about 0.2 inches (5 mm) thick.

Skin grows and is able to repair itself. It is also stretchy. If it weren't, we could not bend our knees, turn our heads, or open our mouths without tearing it. As we get older, though, our skin loses its firmness and stretchiness. As skin becomes less stretchy it also becomes drier. Eventually, the skin starts to sag and wrinkles begin to form.

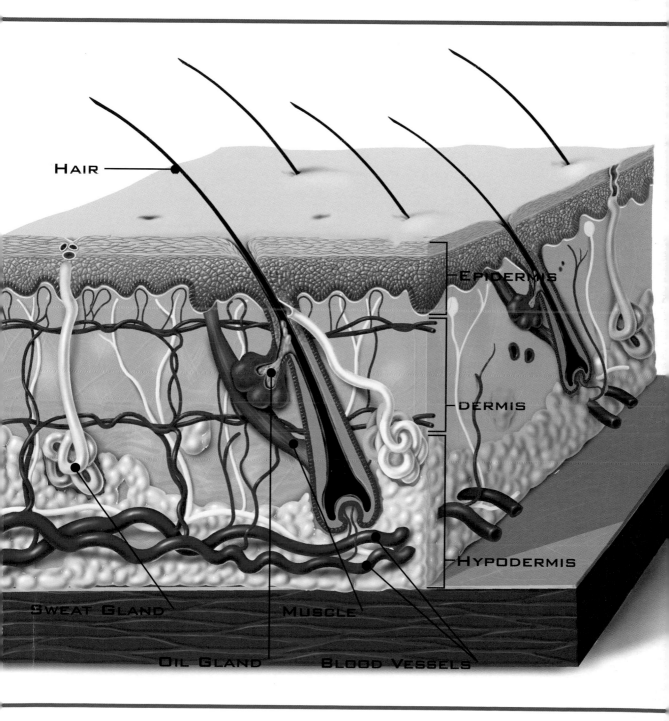

HAIR

EPIDERMIS

DERMIS

HYPODERMIS

SWEAT GLAND

MUSCLE

OIL GLAND

BLOOD VESSELS

If you could see inside your skin, it would look something like this.

CHAPTER THREE

THE EPIDERMIS

I n most areas of the body, the epidermis is quite thin.

However, in those areas where the skin gets rubbed a lot, it is thicker. On the palms of the hands and the soles of the feet, the epidermis is especially thick.

Several layers of cells make up the epidermis. Cells on the bottom layer are constantly splitting

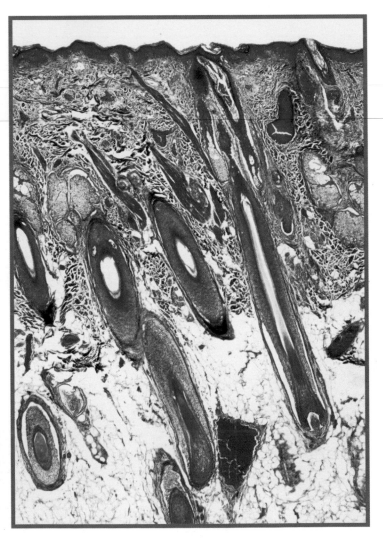

This is how skin looks when seen through a microscope.

in two. This increases their number, but it doesn't make that layer grow any larger. Instead, the new cells move upward and out of the way, so even newer cells can form beneath them. Over time, the cells move all the way to the top surface of the skin, where they die and flake off. If you rub a piece of black cloth roughly over your skin, you can see white, flaky dead cells on the cloth.

It takes more than a month for brand new cells to move to the surface and die. But if the skin gets cut or scraped, things speed up. Cells at the bottom layer start splitting very fast, and the new cells move up toward the surface quickly. This is how the skin heals itself.

In the epidermis, about one cell in twenty is a special type of cell. It contains a **pigment** called melanin (MEL-uh-nin),

which gives skin its color.

People of all races have about

the same number of melanin-

containing cells. However,

the amount of melanin in

the cells varies. People with

light skin have very little

melanin, while those with

darker skin have much more.

Spending time in the sun can

make the skin darken. This

is because sunlight causes

pigment cells to produce

more melanin.

When you spend time in the sun, the pigment cells in your epidermis make more melanin.

Melanin not only gives your skin color, it also colors your hair. At the root of a single strand of hair are several cells containing melanin. As each hair is formed, the melanin goes right into it. The more melanin that is present, the darker the hair color. Blondes have a little melanin, while people with black hair have a lot. Those with reddish hair have melanin that contains iron.

About one person in 20,000 is unable to produce this pigment and is affected by albinism (AL-bih-nih-zum). Such people have very pale skin and white hair that lasts their entire lives.

As people grow older, the amount of melanin in their hair usually decreases. They eventually develop gray or white hair. You may have heard tales of people whose hair turned white overnight, but this could never happen. Once the melanin is inside the hair, it's there to stay.

CHAPTER FOUR

THE DERMIS AND HYPODERMIS

Like the epidermis, the dermis is thickest on the palms and soles and thinnest on the eyelids. Cells in the dermis hold water and **nutrients.** There are also tough fibers that give the skin its strength, and elastic fibers that make the skin stretchy. Nerve endings and small blood vessels lie in the dermis as well. The millions of nerve endings detect changes in the environment. They sense heat, cold, touch, pressure, and pain.

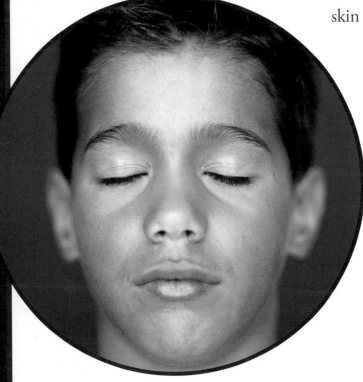

The skin on your eyelids is very thin.

*Do you ever blush when you are embarrassed? That red color in your cheeks
is a result of more blood flowing through the blood vessels in your dermis.*

Blood vessels in the dermis bring oxygen and nutrients to the

skin. They also carry away carbon dioxide and other waste materials.

Blood flowing through the vessels helps give skin its color. Sometimes

when a person is embarrassed, the blood vessels in the dermis of the

face widen, and more blood flows through. The person's face becomes

red, and the person is said to be blushing.

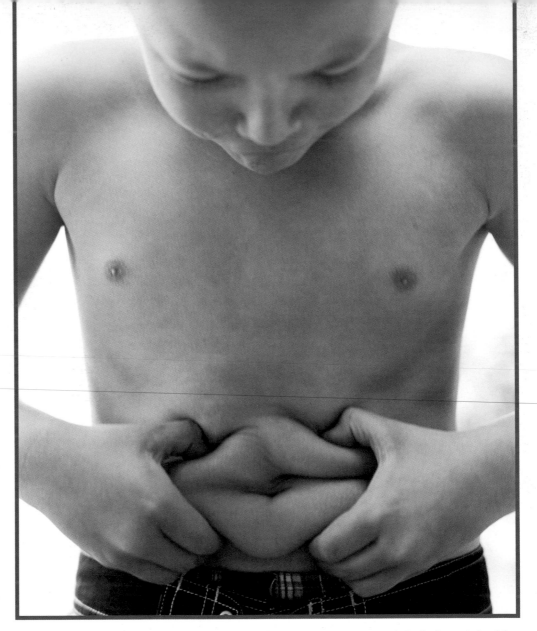

The fatty layer of your skin is called the hypodermis. Having too much body fat isn't healthy. But our bodies need some fat to help cushion us when we fall and to help keep us warm.

Underneath the dermis is a layer of fat and tough fibers. It also contains blood vessels and nerves. This fatty hypodermis cushions the body and **insulates** it.

Months before you were born, your skin layers had formed. Hairs, nails, and glands were already in place. Even your fingerprints were present.

Fingerprints form while the dermis and epidermis are developing. As the upper surface of the dermis grows, it becomes uneven. In the palms of the hands and the soles of the feet, the dermis grows into ridges and valleys. The developing epidermis (which lies right above the dermis) simply follows the pattern of the dermis beneath it. As a result, ridges and valleys appear on the skin of the palms and soles. These patterns are especially obvious on the pads of our fingers. We call them fingerprints.

In 1823, a scientist named Johannes Purkinje wrote a paper about fingerprints. He noted that there were only nine main fingerprint patterns and that all prints fell into these nine groups. The groups included different kinds of patterns, including various arches, whorls, and loops. Although he described the major fingerprint patterns, he did not realize that everyone had different prints.

About thirty years later, a British government worker named Sir William Herschel became interested in fingerprints. He began asking people to leave their inky fingerprints on government papers. He used these prints as sort of an official stamp. But he soon realized that no two people had exactly the same fingerprints. He started using fingerprints as a way to identify people.

Years later, a British scientist named Sir Francis Galton began

studying fingerprint ridges and patterns in great detail. In 1892, he published a book in which he said that fingerprints do not change from birth to death. He also stated that no two people have the same fingerprints—not even identical twins. Since that time, the truth of these state-ments has been proven over and over.

Galton (above) figured that the chance of two people having the same fingerprints was about 64 billion to one. Today, scientists think the chances are even less than that. Your fingerprints show that you are truly one of a kind!

CHAPTER FIVE

NAILS, HAIR, AND GLANDS

The skin has special structures growing from it—sweat glands, oil glands, nails, and hairs. These special structures are referred to as the skin's appendages (uh-PEN-duh-jiz). The skin, together with its appendages, is often called the integumentary (in-TEG-yoo-MEN-tuh-ree) system.

A nail grows from an area called the nail

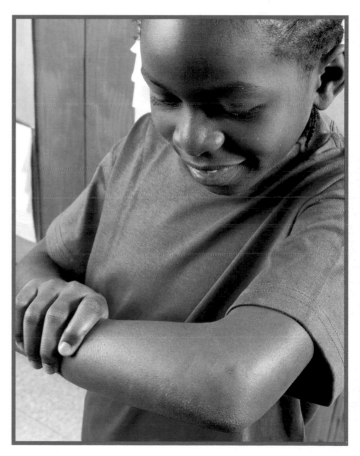

If you look closely at the skin on your arms and hands, you will probably see lots of tiny hairs. Your fingernails are easy to see. You won't be able to see your sweat glands and oil glands though. They are under the surface of your skin.

root, which is covered by a fold of skin. As the nail grows forward from the root, its cells die and become hard. The **visible** part of the nail is therefore made up of dead material. Nails grow about 0.04 inches (1 mm) every 10 days. They grow faster in the summer than in the winter, and fingernails grow faster than toenails.

The roots of hairs are deep inside the dermis. At its base, each hair widens into a bulb. Cells of the bulb are constantly splitting and growing. As they do this, the cells move upward in the shape of a column. The column passes through the epidermis, then to the outside of the skin, where we see it as a hair. By the time the hair is visible, all of its cells have died.

Normally, hairs come out of the skin at an angle. Every hair has a small muscle attached to it, deep in the dermis. When a person is surprised, shocked, cold, or afraid, these little muscles

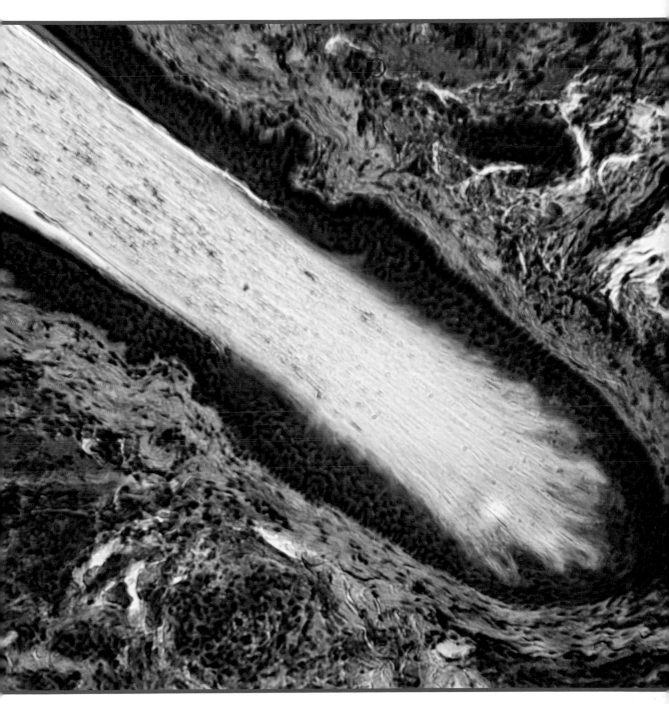

*Hair begins growing deep inside your skin. As the cells in the bulb split
and grow, they push older cells up to the surface of the skin.*

contract, or shorten. As they do so, they pull on the hairs and

cause them to stand straight up. This pushes the nearby epidermis

into little bumps. We sometimes call these goose bumps.

Do you ever get goose bumps? The next time it happens you can say to your friends,
"Hey, look! The tiny muscles attached to my hairs are contracting."

Just under the skin's surface, tiny oil glands are connected to each hair. These glands are little pockets that produce an oily material called sebum (SEE-bum). The sebum keeps the hair and the skin around the hair from drying out. If the sebum is blocked from draining to the surface of the skin, though, then germs can begin to grow. This is how pimples form. Sebum also contains materials that protect the skin from certain infections. Every hair has at least two oil glands. Only a few places on the body—the lips, for instance—have oil glands without hairs.

Sweat glands are little coiled tubes in the dermis. They produce a salty liquid that contains waste materials produced by the skin. Some sweat glands release liquid onto hairs, like the oil glands do. But most open right onto the surface of the skin. If you use a strong magnifying glass, you can see these openings on the ridges of the palm of your hand.

CHAPTER SIX

WHAT DOES THE SKIN DO?

The skin has many jobs, and most of them have to do with protection. Skin keeps dirt, germs, and poisons from getting into the body. Even when invaders do get into the skin, special skin cells attack and destroy them.

Skin also protects the body by helping it to stay at the right temperature. When the body gets too hot or too cold, it cannot function properly and a person feels sick. The fat layer of the hypodermis is especially good for keeping the body warm. But the blood vessels and sweat glands stop the body from becoming *too* warm.

When a person works hard, exercises, or gets an infection, the body heats up. When this happens, the skin tries to cool everything down. Blood vessels in the dermis widen, allowing more blood to flow

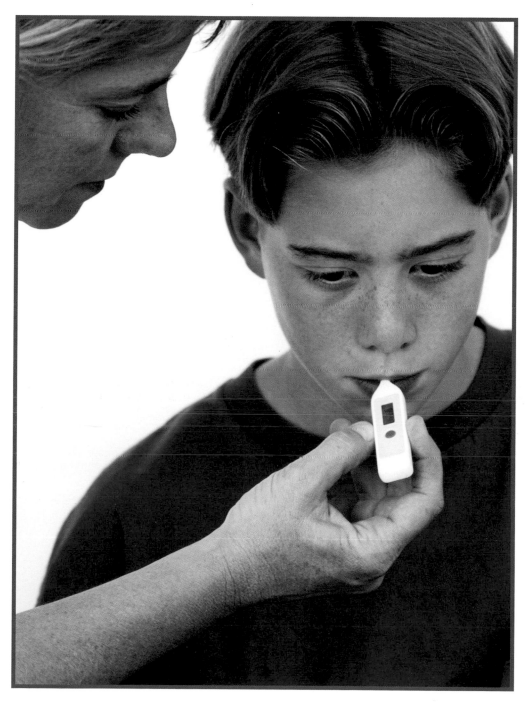

A thermometer can be used to measure your body's temperature. A body temperature of about 98.6 degrees Fahrenheit (37 degrees Celsius) is considered normal.

through. The extra flow of warm blood makes the skin feel warm. This is how the body gives off heat. At the same time, sweat glands pour out their liquid onto the skin's surface. This cools the skin. As the

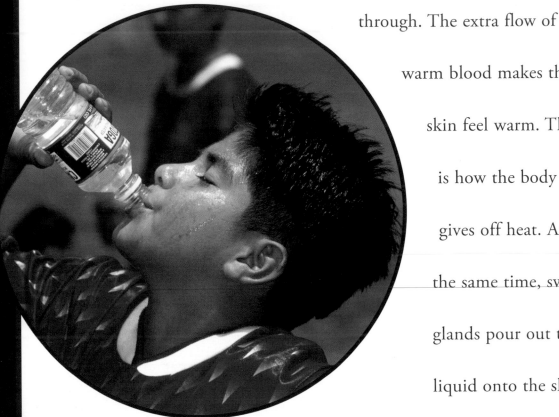

Sweating is your body's way of trying to cool down when you are working hard. Be sure to drink plenty of water when you play soccer or other sports. That will help replace the water your body loses when you sweat.

sweat **evaporates,** it cools even more.

Skin is certainly an amazing organ. It is both tough and soft. It can be hairy or smooth. It keeps us from overheating and protects us from freezing. We surely could not live without it!

Keeping your skin clean will help it—and you—stay healthy.

Glossary

environment (en-VYE-ruhn-muhnt) An environment is made up of the things that surround a person, such as the air, soil, and water. Skin separates the inside of the body from the outside environment.

evaporates (i-VAP-uh-rates) Something that evaporates turns from liquid into vapor, or dries out. Skin cools as sweat evaporates.

glands (GLANDS) Glands are organs that either create bodily chemicals or help such chemicals to leave the body. Sweat glands are located in the dermis.

insulates (IN-suh-lates) Something that insulates an object keeps it cool or warm. The hypodermis insulates the body.

nutrients (NOO-tree-uhntz) Nutrients are found in food and are necessary for life and growth. Cells in the dermis hold nutrients.

organ (OR-guhn) An organ is a body part that performs a certain job. The largest organ of the body is skin.

pigment (PIG-muhnt) A pigment is a substance that gives color to something. Melanin is a pigment.

visible (VIZ-uh-buhl) Something that is visible can be seen. Dead material makes up the visible part of our nails.

Questions and Answers
about the Skin

Once, when I got a shot at the doctor's office, the nurse told me that the needle had to go just under the skin, and not into it. Why is that? The nurse knew that the needle had to get into the hypodermis, where the tissue is loose and spongy. Medicine can spread and be easily absorbed in this layer.

Why do I get blisters on my hands every time I rake leaves or do other hard work? Tiny bonds exist between the cells in the skin. These help hold the cells and cell layers together. When people do rough work with their hands, those bonds are pulled apart. Quite often, part of a whole layer of cells is pulled away from the layer beneath it. Open spaces that form between these layers fill with fluid from nearby cells. This causes a blister.

Why don't identical twins have identical fingerprints? Twins receive their basic fingerprint patterns from their parents. But months before they are born, other things come into play. How the babies move their hands, whether they suck on their fingers, and how they respond to their mother's movements all affect their fingerprints.

Did You Know?

- Doctors often speak of first-, second-, and third-degree burns on the skin. A first-degree burn damages only the epidermis. A second-degree burn damages the epidermis and the dermis. In a third-degree burn, the tissue under the dermis is also damaged.

- A special type of sweat gland exists only in the ear. It releases a material that mixes with the oil from oil glands. This mixture is called earwax.

- On the human scalp, there are between 100,000 and 150,000 hairs. Each one grows about 5 to 6 inches (13 to 15 centimeters) every year.

How to Learn More
about the Skin

At the Library

Breidahl, Harry. *The Zoo on You: Life on Human Skin.*
Langhorne, Pa.: Chelsea House Publications, 2001.

Goode, Katherine. *Skin and Hair.* Woodbridge,
Conn.: Blackbirch Press, 2000.

On the Web

Visit our home page for lots of links about the skin:
http://www.childsworld.com/links
Note to Parents, Teachers, and Librarians: We routinely verify our
Web links to make sure they're safe, active sites—so encourage
your readers to check them out!

Through the Mail or by Phone

AMERICAN ACADEMY
OF DERMATOLOGY
1350 I Street NW, Suite 870
Washington, DC 20005
202/842-3555

NATIONAL PSORIASIS FOUNDATION
6600 SW 92nd Avenue, Suite 300
Portland, OR 97223-7195
800/723-9166

NATIONAL ROSACEA SOCIETY
800 S. Northwest Highway, Suite 200
Barrington, IL 60010
888/662-5874

NATIONAL VITILIGO FOUNDATION
700 Olympic Circle Plaza, Suite 404
Tyler, TX 75701
903/595-3713

Common Skin Disorders

Acne (AK-nee) is a problem that involves the oil glands. Dirt, oil, and germs get stuck in the glands, causing them to become infected and swell up. Acne is more often a problem in teens than it is in children or adults. Acne can often be treated with certain creams and ointments. In very severe cases, doctors sometimes prescribe pills.

Eczema (EK-suh-muh) is a disease in which the skin becomes red, dry, and cracked. In some cases, it may even bleed or feel hot. Eczema is usually found on a person's hands, elbows, knees, and lower legs, but it can occur in other areas, as well. Scientists think eczema may be caused by allergies or by coming in contact with some chemicals. Certain creams and ointments can sometimes be used to treat eczema.

Psoriasis (sore-EYE-uh-siss) is a condition that scientists believe is related to a person's immune system. They think the immune system sends incorrect signals that cause skin cells to grow too fast. This leads to clumps of raised red skin that are covered by white flakes. These clumps are usually found on the scalp, knees, elbows, hands, feet, and lower back, and often itch and swell. Psoriasis can often be treated with certain pills, shots, or ointments.

Ringworm is not actually caused by worms, but by a fungus. Ringworm looks like a small red ring and often occurs on the neck or scalp. It can be easily treated with a special cream or ointment that kills fungus.

Rosacea (rose-AY-sha) is a disease that causes a person's face to appear red and swollen. People with rosacea may seem to blush or flush easily. Scientists aren't sure what causes rosacea, but they believe it might be related to a person's immune system, bacteria, the swelling of blood vessels, or even tiny relatives of spiders called mites. Rosacea can sometimes be treated using ointments, antibiotics, or surgery.

Vitiligo (vit-uh-LY-go) is a disorder in which some of the melanin-producing cells stop making pigment. When this happens, patches of skin become white. This usually occurs on the face, neck, hands, and arms. Vitiligo can sometimes be treated using ointments and vitamin pills.

Index

albinism, 13
appendages, 19

blood vessels, 14, 15, 24
blushing, 15

cells, 4–6, 10–12, 20, 24

dead cells, 4–5, 11, 20
dermis, 8, 14, 17, 20, 23
dryness, 8, 23

embarrassment, 15
epidermis, 8, 10, 17, 20, 22
eyelids, 8, 14

fat, 8, 16, 24
feeling, 7, 14
feet, 10, 14, 17
fibers, 14, 16
fingernails, 19–20
fingerprints, 17–18

Galton, Sir Francis, 17–18

glands, 19, 23, 24, 26
goose bumps, 22
growth, 8, 17, 19–20

hair, 13, 19, 20, 22, 23
hands, 10, 14, 17, 23
healing, 8, 11
Herschel, Sir William, 17
hypodermis, 8, 16, 24

infections, 7, 23, 24
insulation, 16, 24
integumentary system, 19

layers, 8

melanin, 11–12, 13
muscles, 20

nail root, 19–20
nails, 19–20
nerves, 14
nutrients, 14, 15

oil glands, 19, 23
organs, 7
oxygen, 15

palms, 10, 14, 17, 23
pigment, 11–12, 13
pimples, 23
Purkinje, Johannes, 17

repair, 8, 11

sebum, 23
soles, 10, 14, 17
stretchiness, 8, 14
sunlight, 12
sweat glands, 19, 23, 24, 26

temperature, 8, 24, 26
thickness, 8, 10
tissues, 7
toenails, 19–20

waste, 8
wrinkles, 4, 5, 6, 8

About the Author

Susan H. Gray has a bachelor's and a master's degree in zoology, and has taught college-level anatomy and physiology courses. In her twenty-five years as an author, she has written many medical articles, grant proposals, and children's books. Ms. Gray enjoys gardening, traveling, and playing the piano and organ. She has traveled twice to the Russian Far East to give organ workshops to church musicians. She also works extensively with American and Russian friends to develop medical and social service programs for Vladivostok, Russia. Ms. Gray and her husband, Michael, live in Cabot, Arkansas.